MY LIFE THEN AND NOW

Tinka Dorsey

Trinity Writing and Publishing, LLC

Frisco, Texas, USA

TrinityWritingAndPublishing.com

ISBNs are as follows:

Soft Copy 978-1-969749-41-4

eBook

My Life Then and Now

To all the suffering and recovery addicts, and lost souls.

Hebrews 11:11 (KJV)

"Through faith also Sara herself received strength to conceive seed, and was delivered of a child when she was past age, because she judged him faithful who had promised."

Philippians 4:13 (KJV)

"I can do all things through Christ which strengtheneth me."

Jeremiah 29:11 (KJV)

"For I know the thoughts that I think toward you, saith the LORD, thoughts of peace, and not of evil, to give you an expected end."

Love,

Tinka Dorsey

Table of Contents

Dedication

First and foremost, I give all praises to God. To God be the glory! I thank Him for His grace, mercy, and the strength that carried me through every season of my life.

I also dedicate this book to my family, whose love and support have meant everything to me.

To my firstborn, Le'antrinette (Tata) Eakles, thank you for always standing by my side through both the good and the difficult times. You never gave up on me and always believed in me, even when I struggled to believe in myself.

To my second-born baby, thank you for always telling it like it is — speaking truth from your heart, even when it was hard for me to hear. You have truly been my little eye-opener.

To my brother, Wilford (Bucky) Edwards, thank you for your tough love, your honesty, and your encouragement. Even the hard words helped me grow, pray more, and understand life better. Your constant reminder that I can do it and will bounce back has meant more than you know.

To my niece, Jacqueline (Jackie) Edwards, thank you for being there when I was hurting so deeply that I could barely think or feel. Hearing you say, *"Auntie, I love you. It's going to be alright,"* brought comfort when I needed it most.

Special Dedication

To my seven grandbabies and great-nephew — I love y'all with all my heart.

Philippians 4:13 (KJV)

"I can do all things through Christ which strengtheneth me."

John 3:16 (KJV)

"For God so loved the world, that he gave his only begotten Son, that whosoever believeth in him should not perish, but have everlasting life."

Proverbs 22:6 (KJV)

"Train up a child in the way he should go: and when he is old, he will not depart from it."

Proverbs 3:5 (KJV)

"Trust in the LORD with all thine heart; and lean not unto thine own understanding."

Colossians 3:20 (KJV)

"Children, obey your parents in all things: for this is well pleasing unto the Lord."

Love,

Granny & Auntie

Special Dedication

Le'Antrinette, my TaTa — oh my God, thank you so much.
Thank you for never giving up on me, even when I had moments where I nearly gave up on myself. Thank you for believing in me, for being my biggest supporter, and for standing by me through everything.

Baby, you have put up with so much from me, and I truly thank God for you. Your push, your positive spirit, and your constant encouragement have meant more than words can express. You have always stood beside me, and I want you to know how deeply I love and appreciate you.

Acknowledgment

Special thanks to my cousin Eppie and my pastor, Robert S. Polk, pastor of Soul's Harvest Miracle and Deliverance Church, for your prayers, faith in me, and constant encouragement. Your spiritual support has been a true blessing.

To my cousin, Dr. Rev. Latrese Adkins, thank you for typing portions of my book and for never turning me away whenever I needed help. Your willingness, kindness, and constant support have meant so much to me. To one of the humblest, most beautiful, and faithful servants of the Lord — the Reverend Dr. Latrese "Weatherby" Adkins — thank you for your dedication, your time, and your steadfast encouragement in helping me bring this book together. May God continue to bless you abundantly and grant you the desires of your heart. Love you forever and always, cousin. I love you!

God's Seekers Prayer Line, thank you for your prayers.

And I cannot forget my beloved dog, Trouble (RIP), whose companionship brought me comfort, laughter, and joy through many seasons of my life.

In Loving Memory:

Mama Anna

Mama & Daddy

Cousin Big Pimpin

Aunt Lela

Cousin Ruthie

Cousin/Aunt Mildred Lampkin

Sister Kimberly Walker, AKA Baby Girl

Baby Daddy—Leon Williams

Corey

Introduction: South Side

As a little girl raised in South Dallas, I was born on July 28, 1972, at Parkland Memorial Hospital, to the late Wilford and Jackie West.

The late Annie Bell (Mama Anna) Edwards adopted and raised me. Growing up on Goldspier had its ups and downs. I attended church frequently, and it felt like we were there every day. I grew up around many boys, which made me a tomboy; I always followed my brother, my cousin, and a close neighborhood friend. They played football, so I played football. They played video games, and I did the same.

My grandmother was already up in age when she adopted my brother and I, but we went to church and stayed with a few family members and church members from time to time. I honestly can say that my childhood was nice. We didn't have everything the other kids had, especially at Christmas, but we had each other; it was always Tika and Bucky. God, I love my brother. "We all we got"—that's his saying for us. Bucky and I fought each other, and we fought others together.

I recall a cousin of mine, may her soul rest in peace; she was a kind woman, yet she had her own dark side. One day she said she was my friend, and I couldn't share with my brother. Then the next minute she wasn't my friend but my brother's friend. This scene went on for years. Occasionally we would have to sit on the screened-in porch and watch the other kids play. She would say, "You better not move." Her mother, my aunt, prepared the finest sweet potato pie and the most refreshing sweet tea; we eagerly anticipated them every Saturday. We got ours fresh and hot.

Growing up in South Dallas was fun; people talk about South Dallas in a negative way, but that's where I'm from. We had fun; we played curveball, went to the center to listen to our friends rap, and played video games at Reese Record Shop and to Minyard's grocery store.

At the age of 14, I was hanging out with the wrong crowd at Lagow Park, which led to my time in juvenile detention. From there I went to funky town Fort Worth, staying with my parents. Living on the South Side with my mother, close friends, and my aunt, she had three kids, two boys and one girl. We called each other sisters and brothers. Yes, of course, I thought it was going to be heaven knowing now my parents were on drugs, but my mother tried while my daddy lied, but I loved him.

We went through it all growing up, but little did I know I was learning the street life through my parents in Fort Worth. I met my second-born daughter's dad while living on the south side of Fort Worth, playing football, swimming at Sycamore Park and Forest Park, and learning how to jump off the diving board into 24 feet of deep water. He was a ladies' man, but he wanted me. The girl from Dallas, yeah, they were struck and stuck on Dallas, the Triple D. Yeah, at the age of 15 I was in love, so I thought, but it was that teenage love—a crush.

In between Dallas and Ft. Worth, I decided to go back to Dallas, missing my granny, and I hooked up with my first child's father. Oh boy.

Here Comes Tata

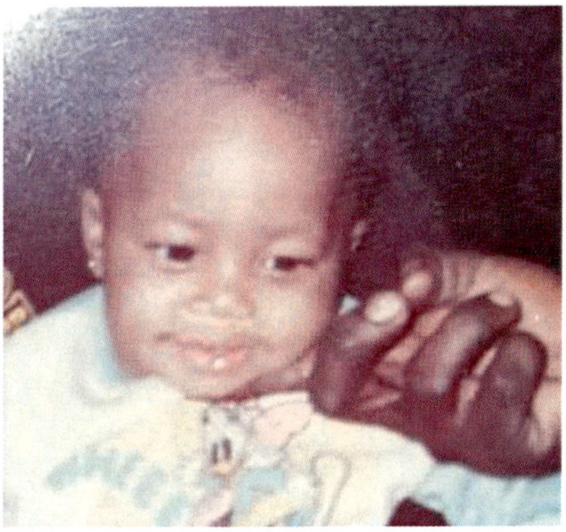

Three years later. Back in Dallas, Texas at the age of 17, I got with Leon, my first daughter's daddy. Boy was I in love, or so I thought. I got with the ladies' man Leon, and about six months into our relationship, I ended up pregnant. Boy, what a first experience with heartbreak, ache, and pain he put me through, and I was pregnant. He was happy, and I was happy and scared at the same time. I remember coming from the M.L. King Center just to find out I was 12 weeks pregnant. Immediately after walking out of the building and going to the bus stop, I started craving powdered donuts, went into this store, *The Packing House*, and got my donuts, got on the bus, and rode it to Hatcher and Oakland. I walked past Lincoln High School, and the whole time, feeling happy because we had planned for this baby.

After my first baby daddy, who taught me how to not give in to a nigga, after his abuse, I kept my foot on a nigga›s neck. I didn't take nothing from a man, and he better not put his hands on me or even act like it, but everything didn't go as planned.

After minutes of walking and smiling to myself, I reached the Meadow Grove Apartments. I could hear the music blaring through the walls while coming up the stairs. I instantly got nervous, so I waited, then knocked. I knocked again, and the music stopped playing.

"Who is it?"

"Me," I called out.

"Come in," he responded.

As I entered into his mother's apartment, I looked at him and started smiling again and told him, "I'm pregnant."

He jumped up and ran over to the couch where I was standing and started hugging and kissing me. I remember him rubbing on my stomach. We talked and talked, so we decided to go together and tell my grandmother. As we reached my house, my daddy was in the kitchen eavesdropping all the while.

I can remember that thin body, all white and gray hair, lying in the bed. As we tell her, she sits up in her bed and asks, "So what are y'all going to do?"

Of course, here come the lies, the fairy tales every teenage girl dreams of.

"Oh, Mama, I'm going to take care of her and my baby."

I'm smiling and believing every word.

My daddy asked, "Are you going to tell your mama?"

I responded, "Daddy! Why are you in my business?"

Before the day was half over, half the hood knew Tinka was pregnant. The word spread and everyone that knew us, which was a lot of people, found out I was pregnant. We had a spot in the apartments where we hung out and person after person would come up asking if I was pregnant.

While I waited for the plans to surface and come true, everything went wrong. He began cheating, lying, and more lying. He told me we were going to move into an apartment across from his mom - but that didn't happen. He also said he would watch my every footstep. But it all came crashing down when he robbed the store and got locked up for 18 years. So, on June 9th, 1990, my baby daddy was taken away from me – he was in the county fighting for his case. On July 8th, 1990, I went into labor after walking on Oakland with my father so he could do his thing.

My dad and I got a ride home. As soon as I arrived home, I go to the bathroom, and I felt a big gush. I thought I was still pissing.

I got up off the toilet craving fruits, watermelons and grapes. I was waiting in the living room for my daddy, and a butterfly flew past me. I wanted to go to the store, but I had to wait for him to get through doing his thang. I jumped and the next thing I knew I was changing clothes again, ha-ha! So, Daddy finally came out, and as we were walking to the store, I started pissing, so I thought. Daddy said, "Let me look." He was high as hell, but he knew what I didn't know: my water broke. He told me to call my brother-in-law. My brother-in-law told me, "You ain't finna have that baby in my car!"

In the ambulance, my dad accidentally hit the button, being nervous and making the sirens go off. My parents had been into it and my mom was at the motel and didn't know I was in labor. The ambulance drove right passed the place where she was. As soon as she found out she made her way to Parkland Hospital.

After being in labor for 19 long, hard, painful hours with no water, no food, barely any ice chips, and a father who was there back and forth, going to McDonald's and eating in my face. Ha,ha! No pain medication, only to start getting my labor induced and not dilating. I was being prepped for a C-section. All I remember from there was bright lights, gently pushing on the stomach, oxygen on my finger, the scalpel, and then I was out. And to wake up seeing my brother, whom I love so much and hurt so much, but he still loves me in spite of it. On July 9th, 1990, around noon, I gave birth to a baby girl and haven't seen her at this time.

I remember it like it was yesterday; he had on some all-white Levi pants, a Bart Simpson T-shirt, and a gold necklace. Then, to close my eyes and open them back up and see my daddy. I closed my eyes again and my mama was waking me up and when my eyes opened all I kept saying was, "Ice, ice, ice," while being wheeled to my room and introduced to my 7 lb. 12 oz baby girl.

I didn't grab her because she was so unbelievably beautiful. My mother said she had been asking for me, and no one would give her any information for a while.

I said, "That's not my baby."

The staff double-checked. Yeah, she was mine.

My mother asked me, "What Mexican did you mess with?"

I said, "No one. Why?"

She said, "He is going to kill you."

Tata looked just like a very beautiful Mexican.

My brother was there every day against his will because, after all, he was still a minor, and he had to wait on Mama and Daddy. My best friend began calling Tata, "Bad baby bite."

By the way, I stayed in the hospital from July 8, 1990, to July 17, 1990, and I checked myself out after my brother's birthday. My blood pressure had been going up during this time and the doctors were trying to get it under control. Deception would happen three months later.

Three Months Later: October 31, 1990

My Life Changed (Deceived)

My life as I had known it would forever change. I was living at the William Livingston motel with Mama, my brother, and my newborn baby, while Daddy was now in prison. He went for car theft and possession, and Judge B gave him 10 years. It's Halloween night, also my best friend Carolyn's birthday.

Introduced to Crack Cocaine in Room 202

Mama decided to move us to the Circle Inn Motel in Oak Cliff, Room 202. This motel had a kitchen, two bedrooms, and a nice-sized living room. The rent was really cheap during those days, only $20 weekly.

I'm meeting people; this one in particular was my mother's friend. What a friend! Her name was Trina; she was a booster anyway. As time started moving along, Mama met Kit, and they went hustling all along with my brother, soaking in our survival skills at a young age. The more she went with Kit, the more chances she took. One day, in late November, I knew when the conversation was about to be bad, my mother would tell me to sit down always start off with bad conversations. I sat down, and then she told me she was in jail. All of the survival skills my brother and I had soaked up have to go into full throttle. I'm 18, and he is 16, and I have a 6-month-old daughter and we're living in a motel. My head was spinning, and I was crying. Mama asked where her friend Trina was, so by the time she called back, I went upstairs and got her. She was already in jail.

When she got the phone and started talking to Mama, she rolled me this glass object with a lighter. She said, "Hit it," so I did 'cause back in the 70s and 80s we were told to obey and respect our elders. Colossians 3:20 says, "Children, obey your parents in everything, for this pleases the Lord." So, after this bitch hung up with Mama, she took the object, which later I found out it was called a stray shooter, then she dropped something white on it (crack) and gave it back, saying, "Go in the bathroom," 'cause my brother was in the bedroom. After I hit it, I instantly wanted more the day my life changed for the next 21 years. Steady listening to this woman my mother called her friend, she was telling me to go score her drugs for her. Not only was she a crack smoker, but she was also a heroin user.

I started going down to these apartment scoring for her; the young boys were liking me, and I was young, cute, a nice size, and a rookie, but I loved the attention, not knowing this poor excuse for a woman was, or at least thought she was, about to start trading me off for her drugs. You heard of homie don't play that? Well, Tinka didn't play that, so I started getting my own drugs. Yeah, buying my own at the age of 18 and my brothers at 16, we were making money. We had to hustle, so a childhood friend moved in with us.

I was in a relationship with this guy from Oak Cliff, the only one I told at the time what had happened to me. He didn't believe me until I showed him; he cried and wrestled me down he grabbed me and threw the paraphernalia out the window, and then he left but the love he was feeling for me, he was back the next day doing drugs with me.

My brother, myself, a childhood friend, and another good friend—let's call him D—we would still act childish at times. We would play hot foot or even throw alcohol at each other, then a light a match. My brother would lay thumbtacks all around, and D would catch them. All you would hear is ouch, ouch, every time he stepped or sat on a thumbtack. But still I was developing a bad crack habit, so my guy friend was still coming around; we would be sleeping, and they done set him on fire.

Dec 24, 1990, The Separation

On Christmas Eve we were evicted for paying rent with one of our hustles, the $2 bill. My brother went to my aunt's house, our childhood friend went to his house, D went back to his mother, and my baby and I went to my friend's home. "Man, this boy loves me," he said to me one day. "Since you won't stop, I'm going to do it with you." So, as I get deeper into my drug use, I find my way back to South Dallas. Remember, what's done in the dark comes to light. Daddy was home on furlough, and then he and mama back out, steady going around Trina after she gets out by this time, I hated the broad. I stopped respecting her and started disrespecting her. Mama asked me one day, "I thought you and Trina were cool now? You treated her very mean. I just shrugged my shoulders.

So back at the little house, we can't lock the door when we leave, or we would be locked out. So, my baby and I are living in the house I grew up in all alone with no water, only lights. I was getting high at night and just when nighttime came, and now it's time to go get some more crack. I would sell milk and food stamps to get a high. Not knowing if I would return home because the addiction had me. That's why I highly recommend if you are in an addiction get help, this was not the end of my story.

I was scoring from a friend from the Meadows, may he Rest in Peace. I would leave my baby in that house all alone 'til I got back but thank God she was always alright and sound asleep. I was placing a brick at the door to keep it closed. Some nights I would make three or four trips back to the dope house, praying don't nobody sees me. I sold my food stamps to get drugs and stole baby milk to feed my baby. Then my brother came back to the South; by that time the only nigga I would mess with was a drug dealer, but I still had my Oak Cliff stallion. Then the more I hung out with my neighborhood girls, the less I smoked. Yeah, we were called the MGGP, the Meadow Gangsta Girl Posse.

We had neighborhood fights; the boys would always come to me to beat up a female who won. Yeah, right, point seen, money gone. Yeah, I got paid to whoop hoes running the streets, smoking weed and drinking that bumpy face (gin) during the daytime and smoking crack at night, living two lifestyles. The worst addict is a closet addict. In other words, what's done in the dark comes to light. So, after a few months, me and the Oak Cliff stallion kept getting into it.

One day we had a terrible fight; he was full of crack and beer, Old English 800. I'm full of crack and kill 'em dead (Kentucky Deluxe). We got into a fight; this dumb dead-ass nigga hit me in the head with a butter knife. He was a coward, so I called another nigga I was messing with down the street in Oak Cliff. I told him what happened; he told me to leave. Immediately, I left to catch the bus; shortly after, he and his friend came and shot up the house, which is a true story. No one got hurt, so with blood running down my head onto my face, I got on the Dart City bus. Drunk as a skunk, so after the stallion's mother came home, that was the end of us living together, but we kept talking to each other on the phone, and he would sneak me in sometimes.

1992—headed to Funky Town

On one nice Friday night, my Ponta came by because his friend and one of my MGGPs used to double date. Well, this night they were doing something else, so my Ponta asked, "What's up? I'm bored. What do you want to do?"

I said, "Let's go to Fort Worth," so we took off down 30 west and reached my sister's house on Crenshaw Blvd. Boy, was she happy to see me. It seems like forever since we last saw each other. It seems like forever.

The first thing she said was, "Carl is home."

Instantly we go over to his house; he was shocked to see me . Flashback - *We got drunk, and I went over to his house. We had sex for the first time, but I knew him. A while later, we finally had sex, and I left going back to Dallas.* He didn't see me again until 1992, so he tells my Ponta, "Say, homie, you can leave; she's good; she's staying." That 52 Hoova Crip came out of him.

Wearing his blue Chuck Taylors, blue flannel, and white T-shirt. My potna said okay, but I don't know my way back to Dallas. He said, "We will show you," but I had to ride with my crip nigga. Potna followed us to 30. I told him to tell my people (parents) I'm in Fort Worth. After two days, who showed up in Fort Worth? My parents with my two-year-old child.

So, I continued to stay in Fort Worth doing good and got a job. Then came the lonely, bored day; my sister was gone, and the lights were off. Oh yeah, she had her own house at an early age; she was very responsible and let some of her friends live there as well. So, anywho, me and Carl were there by ourselves, so he said I could come to his mama's house. Alright, that sounded nice.

I spent the night, plus it was almost my birthday, and I missed Dallas, so I decided to get up and go to the bus stop. He was right behind me; I can remember the clothes he had on: a cowboy jersey, black Dickies, and Chuck Taylors. The Fort Worth city bus came, and I jumped on at first. We were kissing and saying, "I'm gonna miss you, okay," as I was getting on the bus. He stayed on the bus all the way to the Greyhound station. That South Dallas thuggette had him hypnotized.

I got on the bus, and now he wanted a ticket; I got the ticket to Dallas. Upon arrival, I introduced him to everyone. Dark came, and so did the crack demon, so me and my best friend went and got a room at the Circle Inn motel. Yeah, back at the devil's den. While we got to our room and waited on the Oak Cliff Stallion, we started flying, went to the same apartments, and scored some rocks.

We bought about $50 worth, and we smoked Primo's the whole night until we fell asleep. I'm feeling bad because after sobering up I realized Carl is at my granny's house. We hopped on the bus and headed back to South Dallas. Mama let him stay for a couple of days.

On July 28, 1992, my birthday, we all ganged up—my brother, his girl and home boy, and some more of our close friends, and my youngest daughter's father and I went to North Dallas with them as we celebrated my birthday. Boy, we went swimming that night, and it's the night I got pregnant with my youngest child. It was a fun night for everyone.

Finally, the time came for him to leave and return to Fort Worth, and I stayed for about a week longer. I decided to leave, and I moved in with him and his mother, sister, and brother. His mother made me feel right at home. As I'm staying there with my firstborn, they loved her to death. His mama called 911. The paramedics came and said my vitals were good – I just had a stomach ache. My youngest daughter's father and his mother took me to the ER at John Peter Smith Hospital. This is when I found out I was pregnant with my second child. As I was in the room and the doctor told me I was pregnant. I ran out to the waiting room where they waited for me. I began hitting him upside his head telling him, "You got me F'd up, I'm pregnant. He began hugging me. The joy that was in his eyes was indescribable. Him and his mother were very excited about a new baby coming into the world.

Blessings/Pain
Proverbs 10:22

I should have called her chameleon. In Dallas she looks like me; in Fort Worth she looks like her daddy—another two happy parents, but at first, I was caught off guard and was upset because I wasn't ready to have another baby, especially since I was on drugs and my family didn't know. I didn't want to hurt this little seed inside me, but never did abortion come to mind. She was mine, and I loved her; I just didn't show it all the time, but time heals all wounds. I used to love the fuss about me and my pregnancy between my second child's father and his mother because I was a cigarette smoker; his mom would buy them, and he would get mad, but eventually he lost the argument. He thought he won, but she was sneaking them to me and putting them in the fruit tray in the refrigerator. He was an overprotected dad until it was time for him to go pay his dues. So, I am left with his family, who treated me like family. I didn't leave their house until January 28, 1993.

So now I'm back and forth from Dallas to Fort Worth with this precious innocent seed inside of me. I am back on drugs again while staying at the Living Williamson Motel on Second Street. Tata, who is three years old, pats me on the shoulder one night.

"Mama," she says. "Mama, mama, mama!"

I yell. "What?"

"I'm hungry."

And I would say, "Okay, baby, hold on."

I was still smoking and buying crack; my baby steady saying I'm hungry."

By this time, I had probably $1 to my name and a lot of guilt and shame.

So, I said, "I know, baby."

I went to the office and bought my two-year-old daughter a bag of chips and only then realized the baby inside me got to be hungry too because I hadn't eaten in two days. (Romans 3:23: For all have sinned and fall short of the glory of God).

This was my lowest, most painful part. As I sit here and relive this, it hurts all over again, but I know my God has forgiven me. So, from there on, I got high more and more and didn't give a damn, but I do care.

My brother opened his door to me only for me to smoke up all his drugs one night, then chewed the Ziploc bag and blamed it on his dog. I knew deep inside he knew, but the love a brother had for his sister meant he still trusted me; I still could spend the night when I wanted to. So around late December I went back to Fort Worth, living the sober life, going to visit baby daddy number two, not craving or thinking about the drugs but thinking about what's growing inside of me and praying that she is alright.

Jan. 28, 1993

Tragedy on Super Bowl Sunday

Psalm 30: 5, "Weeping endures for a night but joy comes in the morning."

So early one morning I got a phone call from Mama.

"Uvette, sit down! I have something to tell you.

Next thing I know, I'm screaming and crying, so hard my chest felt like it was caving in and my heart feels heavy for my brother. He suffered a major loss. His girlfriend passed away. So, I finally got a ride back to Dallas to be by my brother's side; for him, life really wasn't the same, but he made the best out of a painful situation. He was already on his grind, and there was no turning back. *You might find out when he writes his book.*

My heart broke clean in two for him. He wasn't about to go through it by himself. That was my brother. That was my heart and I was on my way.

It was Super Bowl Sunday, and everything was already planned, but none of that mattered anymore. Football, parties, all of it could wait. I found a ride and headed back to Dallas to be with Bucky. My friends could watch the game without me. I heard later the Cowboys whooped the Buffalo Bills and Michael Jackson did his thing at halftime, but that day wasn't about no game. Life had just flipped upside down for my brother, and I needed him to know his big sister was right there, ten toes down, no matter what.

April 13, 1993

Here comes that baby.

I gave birth for the second time.

"The blessing of the Lord, it maketh rich, and he addeth no sorrow with it." *Proverbs 10:22*

It›s Easter Sunday. Mama has dressed Tata all up in a really cute pink and white ruffled dress, white socks with ruffles, and white shoes. She had matching hat and gloves. I›m in blue jean shorts and a black and green marijuana shirt with the weed plant stretched out around my belly. We walked to her granny's house on Spring Ave. Eating, taking pictures and having a good time. Tata had her Easter basket, which had colored eggs.

So, as it got later, we walked back to the house and ate. I put Tata to bed and fell asleep myself. I woke up early the next morning, April 13th, 1993, to start mowing the yard. My cousin, Big C came by, and I asked him to help me. He said he couldn't; he was looking for my brother, so he left.

After I finish from the yard I went to lay down and I started hurting so I tell Tata to run and tell Ruthie to call 911 because the baby coming. All I hear from the little house to the big house; "Call 911, that baby's coming. Call 911, that baby's coming!"

The next thing I know, an ambulance pulled up with the sirens was on. My aunts kept Tata and off to Parkland I go. It was around four something that afternoon. That evening, man, the labor pains was very painful. I was crying and crying. I knew then this was my last baby. The pain with no medication, family pain meds, I'm on the phone.

Later that night as I was talking to Tata's aunts on the phone around 11:00 that night when the nurses had me sit up in bed. To break my water, they put a pin-like instrument under me and saw that I had dilated to four or five centimeters, but my water hadn't burst so they put a long Q-tip looking thing up me. and fluid ran out the nurse said, Ma'am you have to hang up." I was still on the phone with Tata's aunts. Off to the labor and delivery room. I remember asking for the good purple stuff. They gave it to me and I drank it. They tell me," You're going to have to push." I said, "No, cut like you did with the first one."

After recovery I got to hold my 8 pounds 2-ounce baby. She was a beautiful light skinned baby girl. She was the color of the peach soda. What a blessing! I was thinking about the drugs I had induced and there wasn't a problem with her. God is good! Yes! What a mighty good God! Once again, the labor ward nurses said I had a beautiful baby. True story, not a mother's bragging right, but the truth.

Anyway, we stayed in the hospital for three days, and it seemed like as soon as we got home, her granny and aunt were in Dallas to come see her. We ended up going to Fort Worth. After about a week or so I returned to Dallas, and my baby stayed in Fort Worth for a while. Yeah, I was a mother of two beautiful baby girls at the age of 21, and a single parent. Their grandmothers were in their lives, and they helped me when I couldn't.

1995: For the love of money is the root of all evil

When I first went on Kenilworth Street, it was drug heaven, man—the good and bad drugs. I started out just scoring over there maybe two to three times a day. I remember one night about six times back-to-back, I had a Mexican guy friend, but back in those days we called them tricks and I had him get a room at the Red Door Motel; boy, did he have lots of money. I was really off into the drugs now. I hated for a man to disrespect me because I was on drugs, and especially the ones who was on drugs themselves, so I would get them, like this one in particular. He stopped me one night while I was waiting to get high on crack, so I went and scored for him. He wanted a couple of dimes and a stray, so I provided.

Next, he wanted me to stay. I had a thing about not getting high around tricks, but I had a plan. He finished those; he wanted more this night. I'm going on Kenilworth, so he gets a couple more, but this time I tell him to get two from him and two for me, so I go back on Kenilworth to score, but I get a quarter piece cut into four dimes, pocket the rest, and get the $15.

We're back at the room. This guy is a fast smoker and a real line skitzer, known as "bright light." So now he wants to see my titties. I told him $75. He puts the money on the table. I told him to hit the pipe because I knew after he hit, he would skitz, so when he started skitzing, I acted like I was ready to show him. He stopped skitzing, and I pretended to skitz. He points at my breast. Oh, that's $40 more (no lie, true story). We went back and forth, then another $40.

So now he wants more dope, so back to the dope house. This time I talked him into buying more 'cause I'm tired of traveling to the dope house and it's getting late. So now I tell him $50. I cut and pocket, and this time after about five trips I say they gave me some to sell because of the traffic, but in between I met a man; let's call him Soldier. He was nice-looking and sexy and a sweet guy with a pair of all-white overalls; he damn near look like Teddy Riley.

He asked, "Are you coming back?"

I said, "Yeah."

So anyway, I start draining the guy from the hotel room out of his money at the ATM machine. We started going to different places, so I'm tired and ready to move around. I got about $700 and something from him, and he never saw my chi-chi's.

I go find a neighborhood female friend for him. Of course, I left them alone for the rest of the night and returned to Goldspier to get high, but something told me to go back the next morning before checkout time. He was there, but she was gone, and he was broke. I felt bad about giving him some crack, so I bought him something to eat. Then the sad story was that he couldn't go home. I tell him you can't stay here either, so he leaves. I met my guy friend; we kicked it for a while. We were actually in a relationship, but he was hood as hell—my type. We went jacking; well, he did. I was just riding.

He had me running out of the Galleria mall with an armful of Guess jeans all the way to the bus stop on Preston Rd. He was a hustler, and the longer we were together, the more jealous he got. Why did I let him know about Kenilworth? Big mistake! He didn't want me scoring down there anymore. The more insecure, the more we got into it. One day, I emptied a bottle of bleach in his heart. He hit me and tried to run out the front door, but trying to get out of the gate, he fell over a chair that he didn't see. It was at the bottom of the locked gate.

Because we were outside fighting my neighbor called the police. We both went to jail that day. We ended up in the court room together. He was saying, “Baby, I’m going to get you out. I told him, “F you!” We were released from jail, but it wasn’t getting any better. He hit me, and this time I spotted a box cutter on the dresser. He followed my eyes and then said, “Oh, here, you won’t use it.”

I told him, “Try me, and if you hit me again or even flinch, I’m a cut your ass up.” Let’s say that frog flinched, and I cut him from his head all the way to his toe. That frog leaped to the bed, grabbing his face.

I went to the house across the street where my parents were. Of course, all of the lights were off in the house because normal humans would sleep at that time of night. When my daddy was opening the door, I said, “It’s not mine!” It’s not my blood!

The door opened, the light came on, and Mama started screaming after seeing the blood, “The girls are sleeping!”

My daughters are now three and two years old. I told Mama to hush, “It’s not my blood. I cut him up. She began to settle down and started ranting about West.

“You got to take her to your father’s house. You got to hide her out.”

Daddy goes across the street, and an ambulance pulls up. What a blessing, he was all right. His ego was back to normal, and he didn’t press charges or take me for granted anymore. To this day we are still friends, only on Facebook. He got caught one day while he was out boosting, so now he is away for a while. I don’t know how much time he ended up getting but I did move on.

My granny’s health had been going down for some time now. She had passed away about four months earlier before this went down. She had been the rock for me and Bucky. She was the one who took us in when life wasn’t stable as children. We could have been here, there, and everywhere, but she opened her door and her arms to us. We are forever grateful for the stability that she allowed us to have. She showed us what it meant to be a family. Our granny could be strict at times, but it's what we needed coming up in a tough area like South Dallas. She knew what went on and what we needed, but she also knew what we didn't need in our lives. Our village began to get smaller, and her presence will forever be missed.

I'm on Kenilworth real strong now, all day, because I'm having relations with one of the fellas. It was nothing serious, but he cared a whole lot about my kids and me. Right to this day, let's say he's their uncle, and I love him like he's my nephew, like he's my real nephew. He calls me auntie, but the old saying is, "For the love of money is the root of all evil." There's another one: "You can take the girl out of the hood but not the hood out of the girl.

I'm with Soldier. He's tall and handsome. I didn't want for nothing. At least that's what Satan had me thinking. Yes, he is the father of lies. Oh yeah, everything was everything. Soldier was a very respectful, loyal guy. School was about to start, so I sent my kids to spend the night with an older cousin of mine and her three young children because I'm caught up in the drug life.

Mom and Dad were still going back and forth from Dallas to Fort Worth. When Mom and Dad were in Dallas, they usually took care of my children. On August 10, 1995, I was getting my kids back to my cousin's house. My oldest daughter didn't want to go, but I made them go since it was the weekend. School started on August 5th. This would be Tata's first full year in school, but my youngest wasn't old enough yet. I decided that I would drop them off early so I could do what I needed to do. Because I didn't listen to TaTa, everything started going downhill.

Betrayal & Lies

On August 11th I was introduced to this white woman named Jackie. She was a big drug addict, but she came from a wealthy family. She had a car that I rented from her, which had nice gold rims. I'm doing it big, riding around smoking crack. I didn't know that I was being plotted on by the evil darkness of Satan. His schemes were working through others and myself because of my drug addiction. I was blinded by it and was thinking everything was good.

The power of prayer is real. I have some praying family members that would pray even when I didn't know they were praying for me. I was neglecting my kids but feeding my addiction, not loving myself, but when prayers go up, blessings will come down.

I was riding around all day getting high showing off. Not once did I think to go check on my kids. Later that night, I was getting tired of running out of drugs, so I took the car back to Jackie. She was gone. I looked outside and she's standing on the front porch with a lot of boys. I thought nothing of it and shut the door. Hours later, the police were surrounding the house and Soldier thought it was a drug bust. He was calm and sleep but I'm tripping and high as hell. He said, "It's a drug bust." I told him it's dope in the house that they never found. Come to find out, after hours of knocking that it's not a drug bust.

They knock and knock and knock, so I went to sleep believing what Soldier said, only to be woken up by a police officer saying, "Get up, ma'am, join the others in the living room." I'm asking, "What's the problem?" The police told us, "A lady got raped here last night. I said. Oohh, I didn't get raped." One of the officers said, "Ma'am, we are serious. Sit down with the others. I was furious and scared. But after sitting in the living room with Soldier and another guy for about 30 to 45 minutes, we were led out of the house in handcuffs and taken to the marshal's office for fingerprints and investigation, still not knowing what the hell is going on.

After about two hours or more of investigation comes an officer with pictures of Jackie, and she's all beat up. The first thing I say is "Oh my God! Is she alright?" Then he said, "Yeah, so hold my hands out." I did, and he left the room and came back later. All I know is that he said, "Stand up, turn around, and put your hands behind your back."

To Lew Sterrett, Soldier, my cousin D, and myself, we are being booked , and I'm really confused because I haven't done anything and don't know what's going on—that is, until I get to arraignment. Aggravated kidnapping with release aggravated robbery with a deadly weapon, and robbery. Ohh boy, WTF!!! I›m innocent. While getting used to being in jail I was messing with a female off and on. I went to every aggravated tank in the county – from Lew Sterret and to the government center, and back to Lew Sterrett – being moved around for fighting. I was getting tired of being in the same tank so I would hit another person, and they would move me again. After five months of being in jail, I went to the window to get chow, and I saw my mother was a trustee – she was serving food. She told me to go into the law library. I never did because I was hard-headed and I knew they were going to let me go. This never happened. I remember putting my head in the toilet talking to the men in the floor beneath us. That was a thing at the time. We actually thought we had feelings for one another. Down in the toilet all night long until it was time for breakfast, just to get ready for bed and start all over again. It was something to pass time. Every night, hoping I was on the court docket to go to court. After 11 1/2 months in counting I finally got released on 10 years of probation.

My lawyer came in and said, "The state wants to give you a life sentence." The lawyer returned again and I was sent back to the tank. I was ordered to come back down the next day, and the lawyer was there and told me, “This is your lucky day. They are giving you 10-year deferred probation.” I signed for it and was released.

I told the judge I'm not going to report because I didn't do it. He said, “That's on you. 10 years' probation!” He banged his gavel on his sounding block. I went home that same day, and boy was happy and 100 pounds heavier. My first felony. Three at one time. I was really innocent. All behind a lying dopehead.

I always said if I see her when I get out, I was going to hurt her really bad. I hated her, but my God, my God. He knew my heart. The day I got out, I went to church. It was on a Friday. I was with my cousin Eppie. I prayed and prayed, and they prayed for me, but I still wanted to hurt this woman. Especially after my parents came home later that night.

I wanted to go get my babies; they were three and five years old. I found out they were in CPS custody behind the old lady I gave temporary custody to while I was locked up, listening to my momma. This was a friend of my mom's from Fort Worth. My parents had my children at the lady's house so my mom asked me to give her temporary custody.

We got to the lady's house, knocking and knocking. and she acted like she didn't know where my kids were. I leaped at her, and my daddy grabbed me. The lady was drunk and said she didn't know where the children were. They got in a car with a white woman, she said.

We called the Fort Worth Police Department, and that's how I found out where my kids were. The police officer looked up the address and found a case. He said they left around 3:30 that same day, and I got out at 4:30. He told me that I could get them first thing Monday morning because I didn't neglect or abandon them. Praise God! I called the whole weekend, crying at night and having nightmares.

Monday morning, I got my babies! Now I'm ready to go back to Dallas.

While still in Fort Worth the drug cravings began to come back. By the way, I never did go report, so back at it again, we're going at it a little harder. Every relapse brings seven more demons. To the point my family and neighborhood friends know I'm on drugs. So instead of being on Kenilworth, I'm on Sidney, Cauthorn, Hancock, and Wellington.

Now that I'm on Sidney Block. Oh yeah, that's where my nick name "Triple G" came from - get ya, got cha, gone. By this time, I have had 9-millimeter gun to my head and inside my mouth. I wasn't even really scared, especially after I was always lingering in my mind, "I know my time is coming. I ain't gone lie, I might be scared of Jason, but I am not afraid to die." Nothing but the trickery of Satan and his lies. Yeah, that "fear no man" was in me.

My kids were in a good, safe, Godly home and very well taken care of. So, no worries, not even worried about lock up, death but chasing that money to get my high on. Back in those days I was going to mars - "Beam me up, Scotty!" Because of the drugs, I didn't even realize my weight was dropping from 189 to 119. I was hearing the dudes tell me that I was fine, but all along looking like a dried-up racehorse, about to be put to sleep. "It could have been my mother who was praying for me. It could have been my brother who was down on his knees. It could have been my family that was praying for me. Somebody somewhere was praying for me. I am blessed!

In July of 1997 I was arrested and sentenced to eight years of TDC. I just knew that I was going to get reinstated on my probation. Once again, Jeremiah 29:11-12 "11 for I know the plans I have for you, declares the lord plans to prosper you and not to harm you, plans to give you hope and a future. 12 then you will call me and come and pray to me, and I will listen to you."

Yeah, I was upset, mad, I even asked the judge, "What about my kids?" She said, I don't give a damn about your kids! Get her out of here." Not until the night of August 1, 1997, I was called to give my last four, book in number. I rolled it out, 1997, you pulling chain. Got downstairs to start the process I looked in the mirror; I was weighing only 109 looking like a black skeleton that's when I realized God loves me because he saved me. He had to take me away from my cravings that was about to have me die a premature death. He knew that

August 2, 1997 - TDC

How Did You Get Here? Bitch, I Caught the Bus!

I saw my mother on the same chain as me, heading to Gatesville, Texas. I hit the Woodman Unit first. I was there for two to three weeks, then to Dayton, Texas, which is Plane State Unit. I was very curious my first couple of weeks about being in TDC. For some reason I was at peace, my first few weeks. I was 25 years old and already in prison. Wow, I had two kids that were in good hands, and I know for a fact they were going to church and not being mistreated. So, at Plane State I was messing with girls, not sexually at this time, just with the idea of being in a relationship with a female. Working in the kitchen, I gained weight; then to the ho squad which didn't sit well with me. Because I'm not into walking and chopping grass that's covering my ankles. Even though I was wearing steel-toe boots. I remember a specific time in the field when I was chopping around the peach tree, and then all of a sudden, I heard someone shout, "Boss, snake! Permission to kill it."

Shit, I'm like, what the F&CK! SNAKE! I was petrified. See, you couldn't kill the snakes unless we had permission, or that's a major case. You couldn't run or move out of line because if so, they could shoot you, but thank God, after being in the field for about two weeks before I laid it down, I never saw or ran across a snake. There were always three people in front of me or three people behind me.

For it is written, "Casting all your care upon him; for he careth for you." 1 Peter 5:7

Me and about three more women in my pod that was on the AM- HO Squad, refused work for a week. I later got called to my Lieutenant's office. I explained the situation, received a reprimand, and then returned to my squad before going back to the kitchen. I saw my first parole officer in November of 1997, two weeks after my mother was finally moved to another dorm because she worked in the boiler room. She got her parole answered some weeks later, but I never did.

So, the third week of March, they moved Mama back into the dorm with me. They knew we were mother and daughter, but Mama left March 30, 1998. After she left, I got wild.

I got TDC married to this girl from Houston. She was in another dorm across from me. It made the talk all to the other side of the unit. Time is steadily passing by. I was taken to a holding unit for TDC so I'm being a big HOE.

After being at the holding unit for a while, I started seeing another girl. She was in another building, but I was working with her in the kitchen. See, my motto was "I can turn you on, but I can't turn you out." Because I don't, and I didn't put my mouth where it was not supposed to go. If it gets up and walks away, I can't eat it.

I was so tired of being on this particular unit, ready to go see the real TDC unit. One week after they put Carla Faye Tucker to sleep, my two years in the holding unit were completed. I was then sent to the Hilltop unit.

I ended up where I knew people. I went to school with people from my hood and even a girl who lived with me. I found out that was where the real lovers' relationships were. The girls that look like real men with mustaches, beards, and deep voices.

I was a kitchen worker, and this is where I started reading my Bible a little more. My brother was always writing to me. He's the one who told me, "Get all the knowledge you can while you can, as much as you can, while it's free." So I listened. He was telling me to get my education and my GED, trade in graphic arts, and get an "OJT" on-the-job training in bakery, and I was a baker while at Hilltop. I could bake and prepare enough to feed 1500. But while reading my Bible, Satan knew my weakness at that time. I was lonely or wanted to fit in, so I got a stud. Here it is, November of 1999.

Seven Months Later

18 Months Set Off!

I finally had my first parole answer before I left "Plane State" seven months later. So, after 18 months or more, I'm up for parole again. No major cases! A couple of days after I enjoyed Thanksgiving dinner, I got to go to the LT's office to make a phone call. My mother, who I thought was with my daddy, excited about the football game, was in a coma. I was really praying, and I was in my Bible, trying to wait for the warden to sign off on my furlough to go and be my mother's bedside. Time wasn't on my side. It was too late. On November 30, 1999, at 7:30 PM, the family pulled the plug on my mother, and I couldn't go to the funeral. That was when I knew I had to stop the foolishness and submit to God.

I went all in. I graduated with my GED and received certifications in OJT and graphic arts. I then signed up for business management. I took my brother's advice and went all in. In June 2000, I was on another chain to "Riverside Unit," where I ran into the murderer of the Hispanic Icon Singer.

I thought I was going to college, it was punishment because me and one of the Hilltop Ranks got into it. So, I'm on the medical squad, and it's still the ho squad. We just rode the wagon instead of legging it up "running."

By this time, I really don't care, and I've been in prison three and a half years now.

They called me from my cell. When I got downstairs, there was my mother. I had to be the mother because my mother was too friendly. She thought she wanted to be with this lady, but I stopped it really quick. "Naw, we ain't having that!" My mother had the gift of gab. We bonded while I was there. I had been a daddy's girl during my life. He was there physically but my mother had been there financially. I hit the Linda Woodman unit first, was there for about two to three weeks, and then went on to Dayton, Texas, Plane State unit. I was curious about TDC and felt at peace.

A couple of years back I became homesick. I realized I couldn't leave until they opened the gates. The parole commissioner came to see me; they still wanted to set me off because of the nature of my crime. He said his vote is what matters, but he wanted to come see me himself, and this was in August of 2000. His words were, "Ms. Edwards, this is the first time in three and a half years have I met an inmate who changed their life. I have been monitoring you since your mother passed, and you have done a whole turnaround." He wrote something down, shook my hand, and said, "Good luck." He then said, "I vote yes, but if you were to catch a traffic citation, you're back in prison.

Two weeks later, I was sent to the medical ward. I thought I was receiving my exit papers. I started praying harder. I was already praying for the day when I would get out. I wanted my kids and a three-bedroom brick house with one and a half bathrooms.

An officer wrote me a case. I'm nervous because my answer to the FI-1 case is yes, indicating that I will be released in 30-45 days. He came back a couple of days later, and I asked if I was on the chain to go home. He said, "I don't know." I left it at that. So, shift change the next morning, we were still on unit-wide lockdown, and one of the officers on release duty said, "Edwards, they're waiting for you to pack it up."

On September 21, 2000, I was so excited and nervous. I was shaking, doing paperwork, and getting my scrubs on. About six of us from the unit were released. The handcuffs were removed after we reached the bus station in Gatesville. They gave me a bus ticket, my check for $50, and an envelope containing my Social Security card, birth certificate, and parole certificate, which indicates where I need to report.

The six of us walked down the street, cashed our checks with our TDC IDs, and I bought a purse that went across my shoulders, a pack of Kool Filter Kings, and a lighter. I was anxious, and we finally reached downtown Dallas after what seemed like forever. Okay, let's say I had dreamed of the vision God had already given me with prison preparing me. The little house I grew up in was torn down, and the big house already had its foundation laid. And at that moment I knew then where I was going to stay.

A childhood friend of the family saw me and told me which house my cousin Pimpin had and that I could find my brother there. Wow, after six and a half long years I finally get to see my brother. He got the call I was on my way around there, and he was excited. That's when I met my sister-in-law, "Baby girl," and my beautiful niece, not biological, but she's my niece.

After seeing my brother, I went to see my daddy. That's when my brother started saying what we had to do. Survival skills in full effect. After a couple of hours, we went to pick up my firstborn and on to the movies. "Big Mama's House" had recently been released. I was very anxious and ready to do right. God was still in control.

After spending time with Tata, I dropped her back off at her granny's and I am now back in South Dallas getting ready for bed when my cousin, Big

Pimpin knocked on the door and told me, "Naw, kinfolk, I can't have you staying down here with these old folks. Come to my house." We called it Club 3315. The next day I walked from Supreme Beef, (the warehouse where every ex-felon tried to get a job) to the Social Security office two times that day and still no luck. I didn't give up. My cousin saw that I was really trying, and he got me a rental car.

Oct 21, 2000

I went to my little cousin/niece's birthday party, where I broke my ankle in four places. We were at the Roller Rink skating. Some boys pushed my niece down and when I went to reach for her, then they came and pushed me and I fell on my ankle and broke it in four places. To remind you, I was 240 pounds when I arrived home from prison.

From there my dream came true: I was blessed with a three-bedroom brick house with one and a half baths. I had my kids, a good job, and a bonus – Lol! My daddy came and stayed with us.

I started working at the printing company; everything was going well, then the landlord started tripping. In January I moved my family to Carpenters Cove Apartments, which was formerly called "Bertrand Apts." Everything was going well until Mother's Day 2001. But let me back up a little. I remember the day my brother told me he was going to be a daddy. I immediately went out and bought a pink baby's bathtub with the works. Boy, was I excited. I'm still doing good, so I thought. So, as time passed by, I was so proud of me and what it was doing. I took the wheel—in other words, "I put God to the side and thought I did it"—until things started falling apart. My brother was the one to tell me, "I took the wheel from God and started driving myself."

Auntie Baby Colossians 3:20

Welcome to the world, Auntie's baby! A beautiful baby girl—Lil' Jackie. What a blessing, my brother was now a father - a daddy. We lost my mother on November 30, 1999, but gained a bundle of joy on May 26, 2001. She is named after my mother and me. She was raised by a good woman a beautiful lady my sister whom I dedicated this book to as well.

But after my niece was born, I fell back into the drug life. Especially after I tried going back to rehab. Because I had rent money in my pocket, I was denied going back to get clean. I was in the parking lot with Freaky Mike, crying, and telling him "I know it's going to get worse from here.

I was diving deeper into drugs, not caring, not praising God, but relying on material things to get by. Day by day, Freaky Mike and I separated. Afterward, I met a nice man, and instead of me allowing him to treat me like a queen, I was manipulating him. I was lying to the man left and right. I had more demons this time around, still not seeking God's face, not turning to God like I knew I should have, but the deeper I was swimming I saw that people were disappointed in me, and I branched off.

I was always praying when I was in prison. When I came home, I stopped when my prayers were answered. But the God I know, and who I was raised to understand, is faithful and just in His forgiveness. And He will not leave me nor forsake me, and He has shown me time after time after time. Even when the guns were put in my mouth and to my head, God was with me. When I leaped out on faith and got that three-bedroom brick house and the apartment in my name, I knew He was there.

It was as if I was blindfolded; I still was not calling on Him. I loved street fame and all that came with it. I would give my girls money at night, for them to have their own, but I would always end up going back later asking for it back. Tata got used to it and would already have the money ready to give me. She was simply holding it for me. But my youngest daughter, she lied from the first night till the last night, saying that she had already spent it. Lol! I would ask her, "When? You haven't been anywhere." Did I feel bad? Yes, a lot of times, but the addiction was calling. When Freaky walked out of my life I honestly didn't feel anything because I was doing me.

Back on the Block 2004

During this time, I was on parole but doing drugs, hustling, and I was in and out of church—more out than in. In spite of all of that, somebody was praying for me. My brother had started going to IBOC. I would tell him, “Pray for me. Put my name in the prayer box.” He was taking care of my kids because I was in and out of jail. I was now living in Pleasant Grove off parole and got evicted because I had a fight. Oh damn. Not thinking, just acting!

My youngest daughter wanted to return to Fort Worth, while my oldest daughter wanted to stay with me; however, I decided to have her stay with her godmother instead and her long-time best friend. Tata was 14 during this time.

I’m now lose, not taking my responsibilities living on the streets, spending nights here and there, so I got out of touch with my family for about three to six months living at a motel on I-80, not knowing the whole time my brother and daddy were staying in the apartments across the street. Yeah, I thought about my family and missed them but was ashamed once again.

God will never leave me nor forsake me. One night I'm driving home down Towneast Blvd. I tell a friend while I'm driving and looking, I said, "That look like my brother." I pulled into the 7/11 parking lot, and thank You, Jesus, it was my brother. I waited till he came out; he saw me and started hugging me tight. Then he looked at me and said, "Somebody said you were dead." I know he didn't believe it because with everything in me, because he would have had all kinds of missing reports out. He gave me his number; I told him I was living at the motel right next to 7/11. We kept in touch from that night until now. I just called him.

2005 How I met Benny

I was over at a longtime associate's house sleeping one night. That's where I met Benny. I woke up hungry, and there was this nice-looking, built guy. As I was passing through the kitchen trying to go out the side door to head to Moonlighting, our neighborhood grocer on Scyene & Hatcher, where many of us would often meet up. I was going to get something to eat and he spoke. I spoke back, not knowing he had already peeped at me as I was sleeping. Yeah, the Apple Bottom shorts caught his attention. Of course, the lady didn't want us to have any communication (her bad), so, me being me, I asked him if he had a car. He said yes, so I said, "Can you take me to the store?" Of course, we went and passed the store. *Let's just say here it is 2023, and we're married now*, going back to 2005, as Benny and I liked each other. The drug use was more and more, but everything happened for a reason!

In and out of jail, I was praying more and more, but as soon as those doors were opened, there went the praying, and I know I'm not the only one to *drop Jesus.*

At the clothes, getting dressed back into my street clothes. But was God angry at me? No, he was not angry but more disappointed and hurt. But God did say repent and ask for forgiveness, and He put it into the sea of forgetfulness. So after a year or so, Benny and I started living together, steadily going through ups and downs and more and more drug use. In 2010, he got arrested, and while he was incarcerated, I grew more and more in love with him. We were corresponding through mail every week, but I was doing drugs. He asked me to marry him, so right then I went and got a tattoo on both legs.

From Sidney Street to Wellington and Cauthorn

"Standing on the corner, straight smoking rocks. Aw shit, here comes the mother fucking cops! So I dashed, I hide, I hid behind the tree, making sure them other cluckers don't see me."

A couple of days before he got released in December 2011, I was locked up in a Fort Worth jail. Five months before my bond was posted, I finally got a sentence of 10 months in state jail with five time back. I was getting released from Dawson State Jail. My support team, my daughters, and Benny were there. My brother of course was there. Here I am now a granny of three. I should have been changing my life for the better, but here I am again running back to the devil's playground. Benny and I are really into each other. One morning after waking up, we were sleeping in our van, cars, and trucks. We had three vehicles at the same time because I was tired of walking and running out there for buses. We got our first van, the silver bullet.

Here Comes the Bride/Let's Get Married

Ephesians 5:31: "For this reason a man will leave his father and mother to be joined unto his wife, and they two shall be one flesh."

My daughter was with us Saturday morning. I had $72 to my name this particular morning, 9/11/2012. I decided I didn't want to get high, so I told Benny and Tata, "Come on, let's go somewhere." They kept saying, "Where?" I said, "Just drive." We ended up downtown, parked the van, and went into the record building. Tata instantly started saying, "Aw hell naw, y'all tripping. Reconsider, read some literature." And then she called my brother. Yep, we got our marriage license on 9/11/12.

So instantly, Tata and my cousin/aunt Eppie went into mode for my wedding ceremony. Of course, I had a wedding on the same property I grew up on. I got married. Proverbs 18:22: *"He who finds a wife finds what is good and receives favor from the Lord."*

On October 13th, 2012, Benny and I had our wedding ceremony at 322 Goldspier, Dallas, TX. As husband and wife we continued to do drugs and love each other. I could see in his eyes and feel the love Benny Darcy has for me, and I'm the same way, but we still argued and cussed each other out. February 14th, 2013, we spent the night at the Super 7 motel on R. L. Thornton and Samuel Blvd. Did we have fun? My husband was a good man to me, especially when I couldn't do important things for myself when I needed them the most. He was there and went and got me female things, washed my hair, and rubbed my back and my feet. And sad to say, but honestly, when I wanted more drugs, he would make it happen. But this night, February 14, 2013, he eventually laid down to sleep. I had two stems (straight), and a lot of dope was left. When he went to sleep, I was very scared at this time because of the dope. I started seeing and thinking snakes were gonna attack me, so once I stopped tripping, I lay down beside my husband. I prayed and went to sleep. Then the room phone rang. Checkout time.

I Surrender

Matthew 7:7-8: "Ask and it will be given to you, seek and you will find; knock and the door will be open to you 8 for everyone who asks receives; the one who seeks finds, and the one who knocks, the door will be open."

On February 15, 2013, as we left the room, we went scrapping to make money to pay for another room. As we were leaving, I looked and threw my dope and paraphernalia away. Benny said let me have it. I told him, "No! You should have stayed up with me last night. I'm done!" He then said, "I don't want it because if you finished and I kept doing it you not going to be with me anymore." Little did he know he could have gotten it but he didn't and I was still going to be with him. So, he didn't get it. We walked out without walking back. God answers prayers! See, we asked him for things and don't always recognize when we get it. Three days had passed and I said, "Baby, we got money and haven't done drugs in three days. What a blessing! We moved away, out on 75 and Churchill. I began going to the bar with my brother some nights now.

Sold out

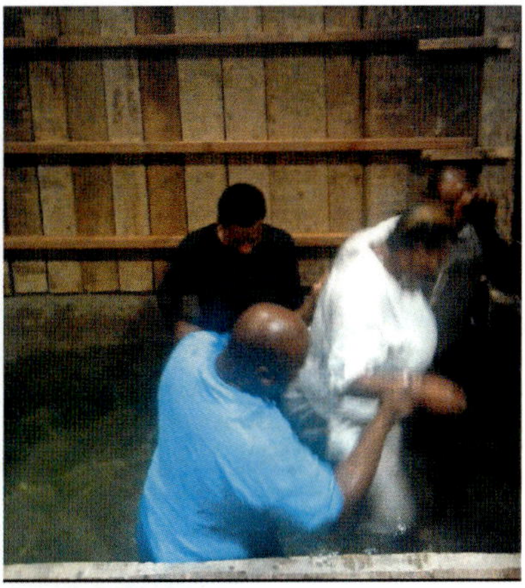

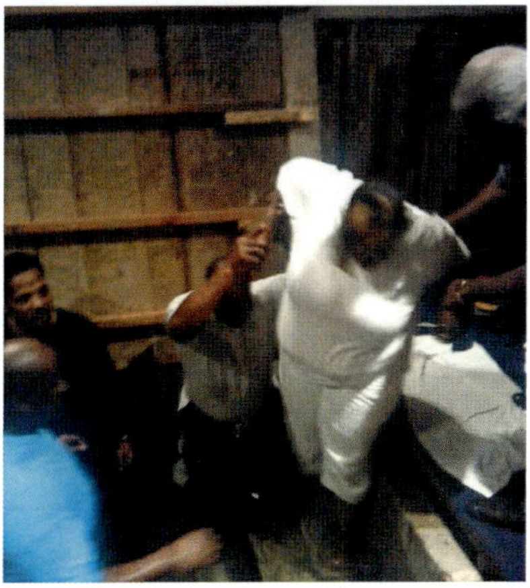

Psalm 51:10: *Create in me a pure heart, O God, and renew a steadfast spirit within me.*

I started going to church every Sunday, getting more and more involved with the church in my spiritual growth and God. I started inviting people to come to my church, Soul's Harvest on Fellows Lane, in Joppy (Texas) to see what the Lord is doing for me. I'm buying church clothes now and not afraid to shout out when the Holy Spirit touches me. Wow, how God saved me and loves me in spite of my past.

Soul's Harvest

Matthew 9:37, *"Then he said to his disciples, "The harvest is plentiful, but the laborers are few."*

My heart is weak, my mind is made up, and I am sold out!

Stay tuned for book two, My Life Then and Now. What happens when you let go of God's hand?

My man, my man, my man!

The Entanglement

How can you love two people at the same time?
Truth be told — real love doesn't divide the heart. When it does, somebody always ends up hurting.

Secrets have a way of surfacing. Choices have consequences. And sometimes the very thing you thought you could control begins to control you. Emotions get tangled, trust gets tested, and lines once clear begin to blur.

Was it love… or just loneliness?
Was it passion… or pain searching for comfort?

And when everything finally comes to light, who will be left standing?
The husband?
The lover (Long live Corey)?
Or was it Tinka all along?

Some truths don't stay buried. Some decisions change everything.

Stay tuned… because this story isn't over.
The answers unfold in Book Two.

In Loving Memory

Kim Walker, I love and miss you my sister. Rest in Peace

About the Author

Uvette Dosey, born July 28, 1972, and raised in Dallas, Texas, is making her debut as an author with this heartfelt memoir. Her story reflects resilience, faith, and the power of transformation through life's challenges.

She attended both Dallas and Fort Worth public schools before graduating from the Wyndham School District in Gatesville, Texas, where she developed a trade in graphic arts through hands-on training and on-the-job experience. Creativity has remained an important part of her personal expression and growth.

Uvette's early life was not without hardship. Due to her parents' struggles with substance abuse, her father sent her to live with her grandmother. Though strict, her grandmother was a good-hearted woman whose discipline, care, and structure helped shape Uvette's strength, character, and perseverance.

Family is central to Uvette's life. She is the proud mother of two beautiful daughters and the loving grandmother of seven grandchildren, whom she loves dearly and considers constant sources of joy and inspiration.

Her close family circle also includes a beloved niece, a great-nephew, a wonderful brother, and a special friend, Corey, all of whom remain meaningful parts of her journey.

Most importantly, Uvette's life is now deeply rooted in her relationship with Christ. Her faith provides guidance, healing, and purpose, shaping how she lives and how she encourages others. Through her memoir, she hopes to inspire readers who have faced adversity to believe that restoration, hope, and transformation are always possible.

In her leisure time, Uvette enjoys spending time with family and expressing her creativity. She also fondly remembers her beloved dog, Trouble, whose companionship brought her great joy over the years.

In Loving Memory of Corey, thank you for your love, your listening ear, and your unwavering support. You encouraged me to begin writing this book and stood beside me every step of the way. I love you for the push you gave me, for always listening, for praying with me and for me, and for sharing your heart with me as I talked about writing this book. Thank you — always and forever.

With love and gratitude always.

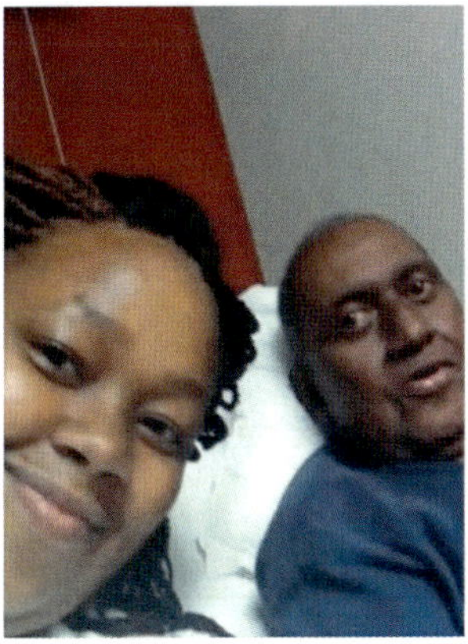

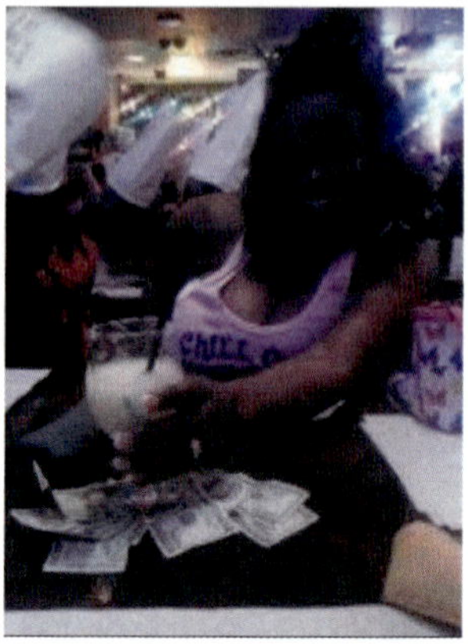

Budweiser
GENUINE

Newspaper Staff

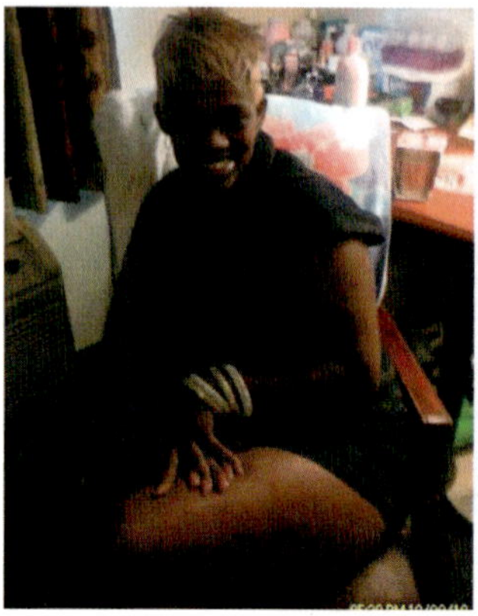

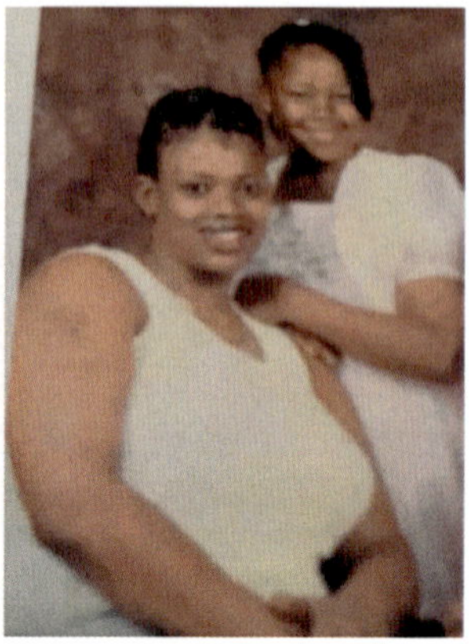

Made in the USA
Coppell, TX
11 April 2026

75180573R00038